SHORT · SCENIC · WALKS
HAWORTH &
BRONTË COUNTRY

60p
£¼
30p
1/20

GW00392240

PAUL HANNON

HILLSIDE PUBLICATIONS
20 Wheathead Crescent
Keighley
West Yorkshire
BD22 6LX

First Published 2012

© Paul Hannon 2012

ISBN 978 1 907626 08 1

*The sketch maps are based on 1947 OS one-inch maps
and earlier OS six-inch maps*

Cover illustration: Top Withins
Back cover: Haworth
Page 1: In the upper Worth Valley
(Paul Hannon/Hillslides Picture Library)

Printed by Steffprint
Unit 5, Keighley Industrial Park
Royd Ings Avenue
Keighley
West Yorkshire
BD21 4DZ

CONTENTS

INTRODUCTION

The Worth Valley runs west from the town of Keighley to drive a deep wedge high into the South Pennine moors, with the village of Haworth as its focal point. With the lofty Pennine watershed to the west, the Aire Valley to the north-east and the Calder Valley to the south, this is a very compact area with boundless walking opportunities amid delightful surroundings. All of it falls within the Bradford District of West Yorkshire, though being largely rural you could be forgiven for imagining yourself much further afield.

Haworth is internationally famous as 19th century home of the Bronte sisters, whose literary exploits played an early part in promoting the neighbouring moorland. Haworth itself is an absorbing place, busy at weekends throughout the year. A steep cobbled street lined by shops, cafes and pubs climbs to the parish church, only the tower of which would be recognizable to the Rev. Patrick Bronte and his remarkable offspring, the rest rebuilt around 1880. The family vault holds the remains of Charlotte and Emily, while Anne's grave overlooks the sea at Scarborough. Across the churchyard stands the Bronte Parsonage, an elegant Georgian building of 1779 that is now a museum dedicated to its celebrated former occupants. Only minutes away is the open moorland from where the sisters drew so much of their inspiration.

Even without the pull of the talents that brought us *Wuthering Heights* and *Jane Eyre*, the Haworth area would still exercise a massive draw to visitors: from its airy perch the village looks over the Worth Valley, whose floor is served by an enthusiastically preserved and superbly run steam railway: this actually leaves the Worth Valley near Oakworth to follow Bridgehouse Beck to its terminus at Oxenhope. Reservoirs and gritstone outcrops abound, as do smaller pockets of heather moorland parcelled between rolling side valleys and independent villages and hamlets.

These lovely walks explores the area's finest landmarks, including Haworth Moor, Top Withins, Penistone Hill, Ponden Clough and Nab Hill. The River Worth is followed on more than one occasion, and other little valleys secreted around the region include Goit Stock and Newsholme Dean.

Most walks are on rights of way and permissive paths with no access restrictions. Several enjoy sections of 'Right to Roam' on access areas unlikely to be closed, while Walk 6 crosses grouse moors: information is available from the Countryside Agency and information centres. Many of the walks can be accessed by public transport, so even if you come to the district by car, consider the local bus in order not to exacerbate congestion. Whilst the route description should be sufficient to guide you around each walk, a map is recommended for greater information: Ordnance Survey 1:25,000 scale maps give the finest detail, and Explorer OL21 covers all of the walks.

Haworth station

•Haworth Tourist Information (01535-642329)
•Open Access (0845-100 3298)
•Traveline - public transport information (0870-6082608)

HAWORTH & Bronte Country

20 Short Scenic Walks

At Top Withins

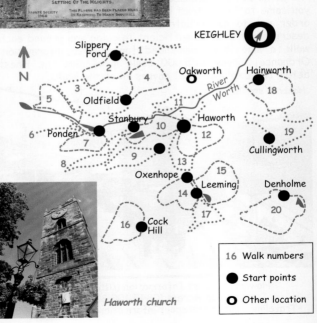

KEIGHLEY

Slippery Ford
1
2
4
Oakworth
Hainworth
18
River Worth
N
3
5
Oldfield
11
Stanbury
10
Haworth
6 Ponden
7
12
19
Cullingworth
8
9
13
Oxenhope
15
14 Leeming
Denholme
17
20
16 Cock Hill

16 Walk numbers
● Start points
○ Other location

Haworth church

A RECORD OF YOUR WALKS

WALK	DATE	NOTES
1		
2		
3		
4		
5		
6		
7		
8		
9		
10		
11		
12		
13		
14		
15		
16		
17		
18		
19		
20		

**4¹₂ miles
from Slippery Ford**

**A fine circuit
of a colourful,
unsung valley**

Start **Morkin Bridge (GR: 002403), parking area**
Map **OS Explorer OL21, South Pennines**

From the parking area take the road heading north, bridging Dean Beck and narrowing to rise past a stone trough to Slitheroford Farm (Near Slippery Ford). Pass through the yard and into a field at the far end. Turn right down the wallside, towards the beck, and downstream to a gate at the far end. Across the sidestream ascend the bank behind and head away above trees on your right. A thin path runs to a gateway, then more clearly on above the trees to a wall-stile. Maintain this line through stiles linking several field centres, passing beneath Greystones at a lower level than on the map. Entering a nice hollow above more woodland, the path curves around and on into dense bracken, running above a tiny side clough to a stile at Bottoms Farm. Advance under a steep bank above the buildings until a stile puts you onto the drive. Turn up this out onto a road, enjoying good views down Newsholme Dean.

Go right for less than a minute then right again on a bridle-way. This drops gently between walls, stone flags indicating use by carts bringing quarried stone out. It swings left to slant delectably down the flank with glorious vistas, and beyond a gate it drops onto a broader track. Go left around a tiny stream to drop to a gate to run a level, enclosed course onto a drive at the cottages at Newsholme Dean. You shall return to this point after a loop to Goose Eye. Turn left on the ascending drive: after a level section it swings uphill again, but here leave by an inviting path on the right. This gently drops to a sharp bend left, past a house and onto its drive. Turn down this to drop right into Goose Eye. This former industrial hamlet shelters idyllically in its deep hollow, focal point being the Turkey

Inn. Since the late 1970s two tiny traditional ale breweries have had spells here, and Goose Eye beers are still brewed in Keighley.

Turn right past the pub and over the bridge. As the road heads away, leave it as it turns sharp left uphill in favour of a stile on the right. A path runs to a footbridge on the beck for a lovely wooded stroll upstream. At an early footbridge on the adjacent old mill-cut you could remain on your path a little further for a better view of the mill-dam whose foot you quickly reach. Now cross the outflowing old cut on your right, and resume up the main valley path. Ignoring any others, trace this as it slants up to resume a higher course through denser woodland, then rising above an open pasture to run on to rejoin the drive at Newsholme Dean cottages.

This time turn left down the drive, past both houses then swing right to a further pair at the end. A grassy way drops left of them down to the left-hand of two gates, then drop down to the stone-arched bridge on Dean Beck just below: alongside is a splendid old slab footbridge. Across, bear slightly left to a gateway at the foot of the steep bank, and a clear path rises into trees. A climb through Cat Clough soon rises out into open country. Pause at the sturdy boulder at the top to appraise the scene then pass through a gate/stile to follow an enclosed path away to join a walled track, with Newsholme hamlet just ahead. Turn right up this, out onto a junction. Turn right again, and remain on this quiet road for the final mile, passing farms and earning grand views to Keighley Moor. A clear day brings glimpses of Penyghent, Buckden Pike and Great Whernside before the road drops back to the start.

In Newsholme Dean

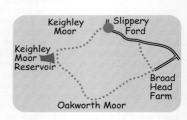

Keighley Moor

Slippery Ford

Keighley Moor Reservoir

Broad Head Farm

Oakworth Moor

3³⁄₄ miles from Slippery Ford

Largely easy moorland walking in a quiet corner

Start Morkin Bridge (GR: 002403), parking area
Map OS Explorer OL21, South Pennines

Leave the parking area on a surfaced driveway climbing to the house at Higher Intake. Above it the road ascends onto heather moorland with the bracken-flanked clough of Morkin Beck on the left. A large isolated boulder is passed, from the top of which Buckden Pike and Great Whernside are in view high up Wharfedale. The heathery embankment of Keighley Moor Reservoir appears just a few minutes in front, and is quickly reached. Constructed as far back as the 1830s to supply water to local mills, it is locally known simply as 'The Big Dam'.

The solitary boulder under Keighley Moor

Opposite:
Keighley Moor Reservoir

10

Cross the grassy embankment to a fork just beyond the end. Take the lesser but very clear left branch, gliding gently down through the heather of Oakworth Moor. A wide Bronte moorland skyline reaches from Ovenden Moor windfarm round to Crow Hill. After skirting an early mire the path runs on to join a wall alongside an old boundary stone defaced by a modern waymark. With a row of parallel grouse butts to the right, this is followed for a few minutes until part way along you reach an old gateway in it. Turn through this on a clear path rising gently away: passing through an angled line of butts it becomes thinner but remains clear as it swings left onto a brow (as the butts swing right). Looking north a big Rombalds Moor skyline leads to heights in the Yorkshire Dales beyond. Advance on, dropping gently through old hummocks to meet a rough access road at a cattle-grid off the moor.

Follow this (Broadhead Lane) down between walls until becoming surfaced at Broad Head Farm. Here take a gate on the left opposite a busy yard immediately before the first buildings. Pass through a gateway in a fence on your right and head across the field, dropping to an old bridge of stone slabs and a gate in a fence midway. Heading away, bear left to a rickety stile ahead into an unkempt pasture. Head away, bearing left to rise gently to a sturdy wall opposite. Follow this along to pass through hummocks to reach a corner stile onto a road. Turn left for a few minutes' descent to the start, with good views over your opening mile.

4½ miles from Oldfield

Sweeping moorland high above the Worth Valley

Start Hare Hill
(GR: 006381), parking
area at Hare Hill Edge, 200 yards west of Grouse Inn
Map OS Explorer OL21, South Pennines
Access Open Access land, see page 5

Head west along the moor-bottom Colne road (away from the Grouse), enjoying extensive views over Stanbury to the Bronte moors. Just before the moor ends, turn down a dead-straight walled snicket to emerge at Oldfield's tiny school. Turn right past a row of cottages, then on further past odd houses to Intake Laithe Farm, with glimpses of Ponden Reservoir ahead. Just past the last house on the left is a stone trough on the right, and just past that is a fence-stile. From this bear left across a narrow, reedy pasture to a wall-stile, then head directly away from it across an open field. Bear gently right to another wall-stile and on through a gateway in an old wall to cross a tiny stream. Rise steeply away to the brow and a wall corner just in front: a gate puts you in the top of a farm-yard at Higher Pitcher Clough, crossing to another back out. With the farm drive down to the left, instead turn right on a hugely inviting sunken pathway slanting up beneath a colourful bank: below is the Ponden scene in the upper Worth Valley. This grand way slants up to broaden out before emerging back onto the Colne road.

Go left beneath more expansive moorland, dead level and with good open views over Dean Fields. Curving in around Dean Clough the Pennine Way is absorbed before you swing back out to the house at Crag Bottom. Again just as the moorland ends at Crag Nook, leave the road and double back right up an inviting grassy cart track, rising by the wall past an old quarry. Over a gate/stile onto Oakworth Moor the clear path rises gently away alongside a wall, at one point being fully enclosed. A grand, steady rise leads to a levelling out on Old Bess Hill, where the wall abruptly ends. The dam of Keighley Moor Reservoir is seen over to the right. Here leave the Pennine Way for the more inviting path branching right, running along a gentle dome and making a steady descent. At a fork bear left, and at another fork a minute further along keep right, dropping down to arrive at the very corner of the dam.

Don't cross but turn right on a broad grassy path gliding gently through the heather. After skirting an early mire the path runs on to join a wall alongside an old boundary stone defaced by a modern waymark. With a row of parallel grouse butts to the right, remain with the wall as it curves round to the left, and where an old wall finally comes in from the right, pass through a gateway in your wall to now trace its other side. Remain on this part moist course past a sparse plantation all the way to a stile/gate at the very end. Here take an inviting green track doubling back right. It curves left around the moor corner and nears the right-hand wall before then dropping to a small corner gate. Continue straight down the thin wallside path, and level with the deep hollows of the old quarry of Blue Stone Delph it swings left along a heathery bank, dropping right back onto the road at the start.

Ponden from the approach to Dean Fields

**4¼ miles
from Oldfield**

**An interesting hamlet
amid rolling upland country**

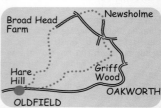

*Start Hare Hill
(GR: 006381), parking area
at Hare Hill Edge, 200 yards west of Grouse Inn
Map OS Explorer OL21, South Pennines*

Begin by heading east along the road to the Grouse Inn. At exactly 1000ft/305m up, the lounge of this popular pub makes a wonderfully sited viewpoint for Bronte Country, though a little too early in this walk! Turn off along unsurfaced Turnshaw Lane opposite, which runs into a wooded corner with a memorial stone alongside a small dam. This pays tribute to the crew of a Canadian RAF Wellington bomber that crashed here in January 1944: an annual service is held to pay further tribute. Continue to a cross-roads of old lanes above Higher Turnshaw, and advance straight on the continuation (Turnshaw Road) ahead. This makes a long steady descent towards Oakworth, but is vacated after it finally swings right for the village. From a wall-stile by a gate on the left, double back on a wallside path above an old milldam. A kissing-gate admits into Griff Wood, and a hollowed path rises to the other side. Emerging at a stile a path heads away with a fence, veering left over a brow. Alongside are the grassy hummocks of an old quarry, while ahead are good views to Newsholme and far beyond. From the brow slant left down to a gate/stile onto Green Lane.

Go a few paces either way and down onto cul-de-sac Gill Lane, which dips down past a former bobbin mill then ascends into Newsholme. At the heart of the hamlet is Church Farm, which in a fascinating architectural and spiritual arrangement stands semi-detached with a church. Linked to Oakworth parish, St John's church was consecrated in 1840: the farm bears a 1670 datestone, and both boast arch-headed mullioned windows. Keep straight on the road rising between buildings. When it expires advance along the left branch, a walled grassy way straight in front. When it swings left follow it up to emerge onto a road junction: go straight across and along Broadhead Lane.

At Broad Head Farm it loses its surface, and just beyond take a solid access road on the left. As it swings left to the hidden house at Nook, instead pass through a gate in front onto a corner of the rough moorland of Nook Allotment. A wallside path heads away, though the initial moist corner can be circumvented by a nicer path. You soon leave the moor and rises gently as an enclosed way. As it swings left at the top, take a gate/stile on the right and follow a sturdy wall up the fieldside. Ignore the inviting stile at the top and turn right with a wall to another corner stile. Over this a thin wall-side path runs through nicer terrain to a small gate onto heathery Oakworth Moor. Distant views look north to Penyghent, Buckden Pike and Great Whernside. Turn left on a grassy track over the gentle brow and down to a gate. Descending past a small wood sheltering Harehill House, its drive is absorbed as the track winds down through the heather colonised quarry of Blue Stone Delph back to the start.

Newsholme

4¾ miles from Ponden

Wild country featuring the infant River Worth and rough moorland above

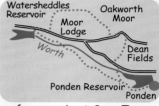

Start Ponden Reservoir (GR: 995370), parking on access road on south side of reservoir at Scar Top

Map OS Explorer OL21, South Pennines

Access Permissive path from Old Snap to Watersheddles

Starting out on the Pennine Way, head west on the road on the reservoir's south shore. At the end it climbs to Ponden Hall (see page 21), and continues more roughly to a brow looking down on the reservoir. Ignoring a drive rising left, go straight on above a house and down to a sharp bend on what is now a grass track. Here leave the Pennine Way for a stile in front, and head along a similar way. At Whitestone Farm take a stile a few strides left, past the garden and on to the far end. Just a little further turn up a few strides to a gateway on the right, and slant across a field to the bottom corner. A simple bridge on Whitestone Clough precedes a wallside climb to Old Snap. Keep left of the house and on a short grassy way to a brow above the upper valley. An inviting path runs left on the bank top and crumbling wallside: at the end is a stile onto a green walled way, with a ladder-stile at the end. Across the narrow valley is Moor Lodge, a Victorian shooting lodge now a retail outlet. The initially faint path slants diagonally into the deeper confines of the infant Worth, which narrow further to reach a footbridge.

Across, resume upstream where the path crosses several stiles before rising up the bank. It runs at mid height through a couple of old walls, and with the grassy dam of Watersheddles Reservoir ahead, a boundary stone marks your brief departure from God's Own Country into Lancashire. From a stile beyond, the path slants up to a barn and the embankment. Advance along the heathery shore path, but quickly leave just before crossing a side drain, and a few strides right is a wall-stile onto the parallel road. Double back to the boundary signs, a little past which take a stile on the left to ascend a reedy pasture outside a walled way. Towards the top take a stile in the wall onto open moorland.

Bear right with the wall: when it quickly turns off, advance directly up the moor on a slender path in a ditch. Before long it fades, and soon a ditch heads off sharp right aiming for a skyline wall much further east. Maintain a straight line by the ditch, moist moments leading to a fence-stile. Across, advance on the reedy ditch's bank, rising gently to approach a fence corner just above a wall corner. Above the moist fence corner resume alongside ditch and fence: the path quickly improves, and as a wall take over the moorland way runs grandly on. Meeting the Pennine Way at a wall corner turn down the wallside path, its straight line featuring an enclosed section. The moor is left at the head of a walled grassy way winding down onto a narrow road. Go left past Crag Bottom and in around Dean Clough.

Across the bridge bear right on the Pennine Way's level course between road and clough. Beyond the trees it crosses sloping pastures onto a drive: turn steeply down to Far Dean Fields. Down in front of the house a green way drops through a small gate to a ruin, then down fieldsides linked by wall-stiles onto a road. Go briefly left to a track bridging the reservoir head. As the main track turns off right as the drive to Whitestone Farm, remain on the reservoir-side way, rising to rejoin the outward route to finish.

At Dean Clough

*3¹⁄₂ miles
from Ponden*

**A largely linear walk on
the edge of wild country**

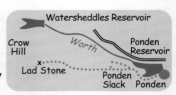

Watersheddles Reservoir

Crow
Hill

Worth

Ponden
Reservoir

x
Lad Stone

Ponden
Slack   Ponden

*Start Ponden Reservoir (GR: 995370), parking on access
road on south side of reservoir at Scar Top
Map OS Explorer OL21, South Pennines
Access Open Access land, see page 5*

Head west on the road along the reservoir's south shore.
This delightful start has Ponden Clough directly ahead, its lower
reaches well wooded. At the end of the reservoir the road climbs
to Ponden Hall, a characterful structure perched high on a knoll.
Emily Bronte visited the Heaton family here and portrayed the
house as Thrushcross Grange, the Linton home in *Wuthering Heights*.
A rough road climbs away from the hall, quickly reaching
a brow looking down on the reservoir. Here turn left up a steep
concrete drive, and when it swings left to a farm go straight ahead,
the now level walled track running to a cattle-grid onto a corner of
the moor at Ponden Slack. Advance through the gate ahead onto

the moor proper, and
follow the inviting
wallside track away.
As the wall quickly
turns off, remain on
the track making a
gentle rise across
the grassy moor. Big
views look right over
the upper valley to
Moor Lodge over-
topped by the Wolf
Stones on the moor-

land skyline. The track maintains a continual, easy climb high onto the heathery moor. Easing out, a major fork swings left, but you go straight on: Watersheddles Reservoir is seen ahead as you enter an old quarry site. Fifty paces to the right is a solitary stone post on a mound. Ahead is a glimpse of Pendle Hill with the Bowland moors beyond, and Ingleborough further right.

Virtually level now, the way runs on past further quarry remains and becomes immediately grassy. To the right is a ruinous quarrymans' hut, while just a minute to the left on the brow is the prominent Lad Stone in the heather. Inscribed 'Lad or Scarr on Crow Hill', best known story attached to it suggests the burial site of a young lad who perished on this windswept moorland boundary: as neither adjoining parish wished to foot the bill for burial, he was buried on the spot. However, as a 'lad' is a standing stone in this area, then the presence of the county boundary suggests a rather less fanciful explanation! It also gives the walk's only glimpse of the knobbly crest of Boulsworth Hill further west.

Return as you came, all the way back down with super views ahead down the Worth Valley backed by Rombalds Moor. Just short of the wall corner at the moor end, vary the finish by turning left at a path crossroads, down a thin trod to a ladder-stile over the wall. Leaving the moor, descend a crumbling wallside to a gate-way, then down between old walls to the field bottom. Turn right along the rear of the house at Whitestone, and over a ladder-stile at the end step a few strides left to join a walled grassy footway. This runs right to meet the sharp bend of a similar way used by the Pennine Way. Turn right on this, above an enviably sited house: below is the slender upper arm of the reservoir. Joining the drive it quickly meets the outward route on the brow just ahead, and this is now followed back down past Ponden Hall to finish.

The Lad Stone

Opposite:
Ponden Reservoir

**4 miles
from Ponden**

**A super ravine in
colourful open country**

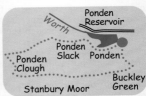

Start Ponden Reservoir
(GR: 995370), parking on access road on
south side of reservoir at Scar Top
Map OS Explorer OL21, South Pennines
Access Open Access land, see page 5

From the southern end of the embankment take the
enclosed track (Pennine Way) rising away, past the old farm of Rush
Isles and climbing as a grand path to a gate by Buckley House. Follow
the drive rising left, soon arriving at a junction at a couple of
houses at Buckley Green. Here lived Timmy Feather, who died in
1910 and is remembered as the last of the handloom weavers.
Double sharply back right here on a stony access road running along
the base of moorland to end at a house at Far Slack. Don't enter but
bear left on a path running the few strides to a kissing-gate onto
the edge of Stanbury Moor, Open Access land. A thin but excellent
path heads away above the wall, rising gently through bilberries in
grand surrounds. Down below is the reservoir, while directly ahead
is Ponden Clough, with its lower reaches well wooded, a riot of colour
culminating abruptly where two tumbling rocky becks merge.

As the wall parts company the clear path continues on
across the moor, a smashing stride as it runs more closely above the
edge of the steeper drop with an improving prospect of the clough.
This leads along to Middle Moor Clough, first of the two feeder
streams. Dropping down to cross a simple bridge, ignore a steep
path down into the clough, and resume on the main path rising
briefly left, then doubling sharply back to head around the rim of
the clough to your right. This quickly arrives above Ponden Kirk,
with an old sheepfold just above. Ponden Kirk is the Penistone Crag

20

of Emily Bronte's *Wuthering Heights*. Legend has it that should a young maiden undertake the crawl through the natural aperture beneath the crag, then she shall be married within the year.

The path continues round to the northern feeder stream, a lovely spot for a break. Across its slabbed floor, to your right, note the Bronte-inspired inscribed stones. The path swings back to the right to leave the clough in the manner it was entered, along the rim then dropping down to a wall corner. Don't pass through but remain left of the wall, a thin path dropping grandly down towards a restored house at Upper Ponden. At a path junction just before it bear left, quickly crossing a track coming out from the house and continuing down to meet a firm track. Go right on this to quickly reach a gate off the moor. Now on a rough access road you drop between walls to a junction overlooking the reservoir.

Turn right to drop down to the various buildings at Ponden Hall, a characterful structure perched high above the reservoir. For centuries it was the home of the Heaton family, and Emily Bronte was a regular visitor here: she portrayed the house as Thrushcross Grange, the Linton home in Wuthering Heights. An inscription above the door informs that the original house of 1634 was rebuilt in 1807. The access road drops down and around the head of the reservoir to finish.

Approaching Ponden Clough

**3³⁄4 miles
from Stanbury**

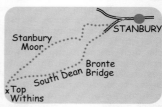

**A literary pilgrimage
across the moors**

*Start Village centre
(GR: 010370), roadside parking at east end
Map OS Explorer OL21, South Pennines*

Stanbury is a lovely village on a gentle ridgetop, with two pubs, the Friendly and the Wuthering Heights, and the Old Silent Inn just down the hill. Head west along the street to the bus terminus at Hob Hill, and bear left up cul-de-sac Back Lane. At a fork keep left, continuing to rise until passing old quarries on the left, the tarmac ends at a cattle-grid onto open moor. Ignore the forking access roads climbing away, and take a more inviting grass path left. It crosses to a gate into a field. Bear right, contouring above an abrupt wall-end and across to a ladder-stile onto rougher moor-like terrain. Down to the left is the colourful valley of South Dean Beck. A path heads away, dropping gently to a solitary tree at the rubble that was once the farm of Virginia, high above Bronte Bridge.

Pass to the right to a second guidepost/path junction, and with the left branch dropping steeply to Bronte Bridge, instead keep on the level one to the right. Briefly between old walls, it runs more thinly on to merge with a flagged one climbing from the bridge. Now enjoy a sustained level stroll parallel with the beck down to the left. The skyline ahead reveals Top Withins with its pair of trees. A solid wall leads on to a spell along the bottom of a grassy pasture, but from a ladder-stile at the end you are firmly onto open moor. The splendid path rolls on, later curving right to stepping-stones on a sidestream then commencing a part-flagged climb towards waiting Top Withins. The path meets the flagged Pennine Way at the meagre ruin of Withins. Your onward route is right, but first make the essential two-minute detour rising left to the justifiably more celebrated Top Withins. This famous ruin is regarded as the Earnshaw residence in Emily Bronte's *Wuthering Heights*. It is difficult to imagine that this lonely outpost was once a home, but whether or not Emily actually visualised Heathcliff here, one can readily imagine her story being enacted in this bleak moorland setting which is, indeed 'wuthering'. A small bothy occupies a dingy outhouse. Big views look out over Bronteland to a Rombalds Moor skyline beyond the Aire Valley.

Retrace steps to the path junction and remain on the main flagged path (Pennine Way) dropping gently down, on to a lone tree at a gateway before a pleasant march as a track across Stanbury Moor. A wall brings temporary company on the right, then the track runs through a groove across the moorland dome and down to a wall corner. This gives a first view of the Ponden scene down to the left. Advance to the house at Upper Heights just beyond and remain on the rough access road dropping away, until soon reaching a cross-path. Here go left to a kissing-gate set slightly back, and a splendid enclosed green path runs on to a fine edge overlooking Ponden Reservoir: farms and fields rise to Oakworth Moor opposite, while over to the left is Ponden Clough. Descend the wallside path to a rough road, going right past the houses at Buckley Green: here lived Timmy Feather, who died in 1910 and is remembered as the last of the handloom weavers. Keep straight on the now surfaced road to rejoin Back Lane to finish.

The path to Top Withins, high on the skyline

3¹2 miles from Haworth

A delightful and easy moorland ramble

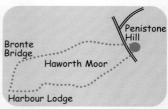

Start Penistone Hill (GR: 018362), car park on Oxenhope-Stanbury road at Tom Stell's Seat, a mile west of village

Map OS Explorer OL21, South Pennines

Penistone Hill has changed from man's workshop to his playground, its former quarries now put to use as car parks. Grand views look north over the Worth Valley to the settlements of Oldfield, Pickles Hill and Oakworth, and back over Keighley to Rombalds Moor. Rejoin unfenced Moor Side Lane on the north side

of the brow, noting that on the brow itself, just up to the left, is Tom Stell's Seat, a gritstone block recalling a local rambler 'who loved these moors'. Crossing straight over the road, a path runs the short way to a kissing-gate in a fence and heads away across Haworth Moor. Immediate views look over the valley to Stanbury, noting the parallel wall patterns dropping from the village towards Lower Laithe Reservoir, largely hidden below. The Bronte moorlands fill the skyline ahead, from Withins Height round to Wycoller Ark. A good path soon picks up for a grand stroll across the moor, very slowly merging into a broad wallside track.

Continue along this past a ruin, narrowing into a broad path as the moor opens out. The isolated farmstead of Harbour Lodge is seen ahead beneath the Top Withins skyline, attendant trees aiding identification as it just breaks the horizon. Across to the right is the colourful side valley of South Dean Beck, into which you are about to descend. The rougher path runs down and on to arrive at Bronte Bridge, a simple but attractive footbridge. By the path immediately before it is the seat-shaped stone known as the Bronte Chair. Instead of crossing the bridge, leave by a rougher path climbing steeply up the right bank of the sidestream boasting the 'Bronte Waterfall'. This slender trickle, no different from any other tinkling Pennine streams, really pushes the literary connection! This rough climb quickly levels out and the path runs gently on towards Harbour Lodge. Passing grouse butts the path runs to a small footbridge, just above which is the unsurfaced access road.

Turn left away from the farm, and on for some time until beyond an appreciable kink. As the road levels and straightens, it is seen for some distance ahead as it crosses the moor. However, a waymark sends a thin but clear and far more inviting path off to the right. This angles gently down, with a brief moist spell in the middle (Leeshaw Reservoir is ahead, below) before improving and reaching a wall along the bottom of the moor. A good path is joined to run along to the left. After a gentle rise Penistone Hill re-appears ahead, with Drop Farm (tearoom) just ahead. Follow its drive out the rest of the way to the road just down from the start.

Opposite: Bronte Bridge   *Worth Valley from Penistone Hill*

**4¹⁄₂ miles
from Haworth**

**Interest galore
in this delve into
the Worth Valley**

Start Parish church (GR: 029372), car parks nearby
Map OS Explorer OL21, South Pennines

Facing the church take a cobbled street to the right, rising past the Kings Arms and churchyard to the Parsonage. Just past it an enclosed path takes over, emerging into open pastures. A splendid flagged path runs through fields to join West Lane at the end of the houses. Just to the left fork left onto Penistone Hill, and ignoring an early branch left keep straight on with super views over the Worth Valley. At a parking area opposite a cemetery a broad track slants down towards Lower Laithe Reservoir. Off the moor it becomes enclosed above waterworks buildings and out onto a road by the dam. Turn briefly left, then take a stile on the right. Cross a field bottom beneath Intake Farm to a gate/stile, then slant up to a small gate at the top corner. Joining a walled green way, go

briefly right then leave by a gate on the left at a wood corner. A good path runs outside the trees, then part enclosed, emerging and tapering to a stile into a field. Bear left across to a gate overlooking steps down to a small stream. Up the other side head away past ruinous barns and along a wallside to a barnyard: in it turn left through gates/pens and an old way ascends the wallside to a stile onto Haworth Moor.

Independence for Lumb Foot?

Opposite: Stanbury

26

Turn right on the broad path only as far as a ruin, Middle Intake. Just past it drop to a stile, and slant down the field to another in the far corner. This overlooks South Dean Beck, with the reservoir to the right. A little path slants down to a footbridge on the beck. Cross a small mire to a wall-stile, then a thin path slants left up another steep field. Rising to an old wall, continue up by scant wall remains to a fence-stile, then straight up to a wall-stile onto Back Lane at a house. Turn right down to Hob Hill at the west end of Stanbury, and head on through the village. At the far end continue down past the Oxenhope junction to a snicket left to Lumb Foot. This neat walled path later drops steeply into the tiny hamlet.

Go left to the road end at the bottom houses, where a track continues down past a former mill to a farm bridge on the River Worth. Use the fine old bridge just beyond, then rejoin the access road in the barnyard. Approaching a cattle-grid at the end, don't use but take a gate to its right and as the drive climbs away, remain on level ground near the river. Ignoring a ramshackle bridge, advance around a tight bank then follow a fence along towards the fine arch of Long Bridge. Through a stile at the end follow the returned river the few strides upstream to the bridge. Across, bear right on a broad path rising above a side beck: soon parting company it rises to a gate/stile. The path continues up, with a sunken section climbing to a stile into a garden. Bear left beneath the house to a narrow snicket, which heads away to emerge into a field. Continue away with an old wall, and as it rises away cross to a stile opposite. Resume on a field top, becoming enclosed at a gate/stile part way on, then opening into another field. Rise right with the wall to a gate to pass right of a house to rejoin West Lane. Go left to finish.

*3¾ miles
from Haworth*

**Plenty of ups and downs
in a double crossing of
the valley's quieter parts**

*Start Parish church (GR: 029372), car parks nearby
Map OS Explorer OL21, South Pennines*

From the church turn down Changegate opposite, to a crossroads. Cross and turn right on North Street, cutting a tiny corner of the junction to bear left down Mytholmes Lane. This descends to a junction with Ebor Lane: go straight ahead past an old tollhouse complete with table of charges. Head on an access road between terraces, at the end a broad path drops down to bridge Bridgehouse Beck. Across, a road runs past cottages to Vale Mill Lane. Go left to a sharp bend at the mill, bridging the River Worth then turn up steps beneath a rail bridge. The path rises to a junction of like ways: go left above a steep wooded bank. At a garden take a like path up the near side, emerging onto a drive and rising beneath an old chimney onto Providence Lane.

Cross to an access road past Lodge Farm to end at a former farm. In the yard go right to a gate at the near side of the house, leaving the garden by a corner stile. Ascend the fieldside to another stile, don't use but go left with the wall to a gate at the end, where an enclosed way rises onto Tim Lane. Climb the road until it levels out on the edge of Oakworth, then take a short access road left into the yard at Oakworth Farm. Opposite the farmhouse take a gate to the right of an enclosed track and head along the parallel fieldside, crossing the track at the end and on through a further stile to approach Lower Hob Cote. Across the drive bear right to a gap onto an adjacent drive, then go left down it to the house side. From a gate/stile on the right a thin path resumes on the field bottom, with sweeping Worth Valley views. *Opposite: Long Bridge*

A stile at the end puts you on another drive: slant left down it to a hairpin, where a stile puts you back on the direct march along a field bottom, between newly planted trees to a corner stile into Covey Wood. A grand path crosses the top to a stile out to cross two fields, and a wall leads to a corner stile behind a house. Advance through the cluster at Higher Scholes, straight on the access road ahead to a junction: from a stile in front bear right to a wall-stile ahead, and on again to the right of a house where a small gate accesses the drive. Dropping slightly to the house, a gate on the right by a barn sends you on one last field bottom to a stile onto Oldfield Lane.

Go briefly left past lovely Laverock Hall (1641): after the adjacent house take a gate on the left and slant down to a gate below a bungalow, then cross to a stile onto an enclosed drive. Go left, keeping left to Street Head Farm. From a stile to its left an enclosed path slants away to emerge in a mini-ravine. Ignoring the branch right at its end, resume more openly, still enclosed. The part sunken way opens out to slant down to a concrete access road. Cross and go down by the sunken way to the valley floor. Go left to a gate/stile onto the riverbank, with Long Bridge upstream. Don't cross but take a gate downstream, a path tracing the Worth all the way to Lord Bridge. En route a ladder-stile on the right sees a concession path enjoy a nice sweep of the river to a kissing-gate back onto the public path. The way remains clear, passing a pond before a stile puts you onto Lord Bridge at the merging of Tim Lane and Lord Lane. Cross and head up the latter, whose footway makes a very steep ascent to conclude.

**4 miles
from Haworth**

**Beckside and moorland
walking with the sight,
sound and smell
of steam trains**

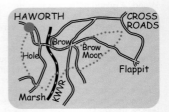

HAWORTH | CROSS ROADS
Brow
Brow Moor
Hole
Flappit
Marsh | KWVR

*Start Parish church (GR: 029372), car parks nearby
Map OS Explorer OL21, South Pennines*

    Entering the churchyard take the flagged path rising left, then left again to leave by a kissing-gate. The enclosed path heads away to a junction, where keep straight on a thinner one ahead. This zigzags up into a field corner by Sowdens. Go left on field bottoms to an access road above Hole Farm. A few strides uphill an enclosed path resumes above the houses before tracing a wallside away. Big views look to Oxenhope Moor ahead. A brief spell enclosed by walls transfers you to the other side, dropping down a track past a dam to a road at Old Oxenhope Farm. Turn left down to a junction at Marsh.

    Go briefly left then turn right down Bents Lane to three houses. Swing left on the drive to Bents Cottage, then pass to its left into a field. Head along the field bottoms, becoming enclosed to emerge onto a drive at North Ives. A couple of strides right resume at a stile opposite, across another field bottom to meet an enclosed path. Turn right down its colourful course, slanting right down to the valley floor. Pass under the railway and over charming Donkey Bridge, an old packhorse bridge illustrated on page 33. Go left on a path downstream with Bridgehouse Beck, briefly, then it bears away to rise to a drive. Go left along the front of the house at Ives Bottom, then down to a small gate ahead. The path runs beneath a bank to drop via a stile onto a track at a ruin. Turn right up the track's steep pull to a stile onto the A6033 Hebden Road. Cross and go a few strides left to a few steps sending a thin path up into undergrowth. Escaping, it rises to a fence-gap then steeply up to a stile in the top-left corner. It improves to ascend a part wooded bank, tracing a wall up to a stile onto Black Moor Road in front of a working quarry and solitary wind turbine. Turning right, rise slightly to the end of Brow Moor, where a broad wallside path turns up onto the moor. This soon improves to shadow the wall over the heathery brow and down to Brow Top Road.

Cross over and down Hardgate Lane, which at Hardgate Cottage becomes a footway. Descending past old quarries, it becomes a rough road again at another house. Here take a stile on the left and a wallside path heads away to a stile at the far end onto a heathery bank. Looking down on a small reservoir, a little path slants up to an old wall then contours (at times thin but clear) through heather to the far side, reaching a mast at the former Three Sisters Hotel. Its drive leads back up to Brow Top Road: go briefly right to the 30mph sign, as Haworth returns to the scene. Here a good path heads off across Brow Moor, broadening and running largely level before angling down onto Black Moor Road. Turning briefly right, a path cuts a corner to drop past a seat, down through trees back to Brow Top Road. Just below is Hebden Road, beneath which Brow Road winds steeply down through Haworth Brow into Haworth. Cross the railway bridge and up Bridgehouse Lane for the village centre, bearing left up the cobbles of Main Street back to the church.

Haworth from Brow Moor

4 miles from Haworth

Shadowing steam trains before a field and moorland return

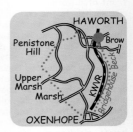

Start Railway station
(GR: 034372), parking nearby
Map OS Explorer OL21,
South Pennines

Across the railway footbridge turn left on Belle Isle Road, joining Bridgehouse Lane. Go left back over the railway and bear right on Brow Road. This immediately swings left to climb away, but leave it by taking a few steps up on the right. A flagged path heads away, along the field bottom to join an old mill-cut. Over to the right the railway runs parallel across Bridgehouse Beck: up above hovers Brow Moor wind turbine. Before long the path bridges the cut and runs on to its termination, just beyond which it forks. One branch drops to a footbridge on the adjacent beck, while yours runs straight ahead to a ruin. From a stile opposite, cross the base of a scrubby bank to approach a house, Ives Bottom. Pass along the front, and as the drive heads away, the path turns right to drop to the beck. Head upstream past stone-arched Donkey Bridge to cross at a footbridge further on. The way resumes past a solitary house and out on a drive. When it bridges the beck, remain on the near side on a path between beck and railway. Re-cross at another footbridge, and the path runs on to a former mill yard and out onto Harry Lane on the edge of Oxenhope. Turn right to the station.

Keep on (Mill Lane) past it to a junction and go left up Cross Lane. As it narrows go right before the school into playing fields. Ascend along the side, and part-way up cross above a low bank to a small gate/stile in the wall opposite. Now bear right to a wall-stile lower down the opposite side, and the path continues down to a beck. Go a few strides upstream to a stile, and a short enclosed path runs to a footbridge. Emerging by the back of a house go left up the short way to a stile at the top, then ascend the fieldside, soon becoming enclosed by walls to a gate into a yard between two houses at Mould Greave. From a kissing-gate on the right pass along the rear of the right-hand house and an enclosed path runs along to another drive. Go left up this onto the road on the edge of Marsh, alongside a Methodist church.

Go briefly left to a kissing-gate on the right onto tiny Marsh Common. A path rises to a kissing-gate, then ascend two fieldsides to a stile at the top onto a drive between houses. Ascend this onto the road in Upper Marsh. Go briefly right to a fork, then take a rough track rising left onto the moorland of Penistone Hill. As it swings left take a grassier path straight up, levelling out to run to a cricket pitch. In front is a massive quarry hole. Go right, remaining on the main path which angles away between hole and wall. Keeping left of further old quarries it runs past an OS column (1030ft/314m) on the left to curve left to a cross-paths at a modern sculpture, 'Literary Landscape'. Turn right to quickly run to a moor-edge road, Dimples Lane. Cross and go down the drive to Sowdens. Remain on the enclosed track continuing beneath it to a T-junction of ways. Take the path left, which runs firmly on to the church. The finish is a load of cobbles! - turn down the main street, and reaching the Fleece Inn go left down a steeper little street: across Rawdon Road descend Butt Lane, at the bottom regaining the start point at the railway footbridge.

Donkey Bridge on Bridgehouse Beck

4¼ miles from Oxenhope

Absorbing old ways under moorland slopes, lovely views

Start Station (GR: 032353), roadside parking nearby
Map OS Explorer OL21, South Pennines

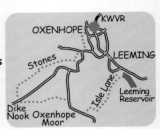

Oxenhope is a fine Pennine mill community, in a basin with steep hills rising on almost all sides, through pastures to the layer of moor above: village pub is the Bay Horse. From the station entrance turn left on Mill Lane, quickly becoming Harry Lane to climb to the A6033. Cross and resume up Dark Lane. At the first opportunity go right on Yate Lane to emerge by the Post office in Lowertown. Go left a short way up Denholme Road then bear right on Jew Lane. Avoid further, lesser forks right until the handful of houses at Back Leeming, where bear right on a level cul-de-sac road. Becoming a rougher access road it crosses a bridge to Egypt House. Ascend an enclosed way to its right to emerge onto an access road.

St Mary's church, Oxenhope

Opposite:
Intake Lane

Turn right, rising between houses. Immediately after, take a firm path slanting left, rising above a house to the foot of its enclosed continuation, Isle Lane. A grand climb

34

between walls has views back over Leeming Reservoir, emerging at the top into open country. Either remain on the part sunken way, or make use of grassy tracks curving more to the left. Either way, you'll find Isle Lane levelling out at the top. Ignoring its continuing enclosed course, take a ladder-stile on your right and head away with a wall, aiming for a prominent mast. Through a gap at the end continue with an old wall, and as it starts to drop away, bear left up to a nearby wall corner. A grass track forms between old walls to a stile onto a moor-edge road beneath Oxenhope Moor: turn right.

Just beyond a bend under the mast, at the start of a steep drop, take a stile on the left. Head away with a wall along the field top (Leeshaw Reservoir ahead) to drop slightly to a corner stile onto a track, Intake Lane. Rise left, briefly, before dropping to the Waggon & Horses pub at Dike Nook on the A6033. Cross to a house and go left on its short drive, just past which it swings right downhill as a rough access road: at the bottom it goes right past Hard Nese Farm and on to emerge on the island of heather moorland that is Stones. As the track goes sharp left, take the path rising to a wall corner to run grandly along the crest. At the end the path meets a track by a house: go straight over and along a path past Olde Croft, with mullioned windows. The path runs out into a drive, and as its swings right a flagged path goes straight on at a path cross-roads: here take one left, through a stile and down through a tiny gate to descend a fieldside. Oxenhope's church is just to the right. A gate in the bottom corner sends a snicket down onto Shaw Lane on the edge of the village. Turn right to the junction with the main road, then take a surfaced path left. This descends through the park to swing around to emerge onto Cross Lane. Turn down to finish.

*4³⁄₄ miles
from Oxenhope*

**A breezy tramp
over moorland heights**

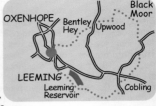

Start Lowertown (GR: 034347),
street parking near Post office
Map OS Explorer OL21, South Pennines
Access Open Access land, see page 5

Leave the Post office along Yate Lane, passing the Manor House and rising out of the village. At Yate House on the right, turn up a lane to a lone house. From a gate/stile on the right ascend a steep field to a stile at its tapering top, then up a fieldside to a stile onto a rough road. Go briefly left, and level with a partially renovated ruin take an enclosed green way right onto the pocket moor of Bentley Hey. Head away left, soon gently rising above an old wall. The path angles up with a sunken way largely to your right, then level again before rising to a stile onto Black Moor Road. Go briefly left, then right on Upwood Park caravan site road: remain on the continuing track onto Black Moor. Turn left on a wallside path dropping gently to meet the Cuckoo Park Lane track entering the moor. Turn right on this across the heart of the moor, a pleasant amble through heather to approach the fence corner of an old quarry.

Here leave the track crossroads by taking one up to the right with an old wall. Quickly reaching a cross-paths in a nick, pass through the wall and take a broad path rising gently over the brow. The now flagged path drops to a gate onto Trough Lane. Go right on the road to the next bend, and a little further is a stile on the left a short way beyond a drive. After a few moist steps rise with the wall to a narrow corner gap into a tiny plantation edge. Cross to a fence-stile ahead, and on to another opposite. Now slant right up the steeper bank, through a gate in a rising wall and resume slanting to the brow. Advance on to a sturdy wall corner ahead: below is

Leeming Reservoir. Don't follow the wall but trace a crumbling one dropping away, a grassy way tracing it to a stile onto the B6141.

Opposite, a reedy groove rises left and on to a corner on the brow. Continue away over Sentry Hill, the walk's high point at 1207ft/368m. From a stile opposite turn right down an enclosed way onto a road at Cobling Farm. Go left on the continuing rough lane to its terminus at a surfaced access road. Don't join it however, but from a gate on your right a grass track descends Open Access land to a wall corner, and down with the wall to approach a house. Don't use the gate at the bottom but take one just left, from where a grass track resumes dropping left with a wall to level out. Here turn left to trace a conduit as far as a bridge on it, where a ladder-stile brings in the Bronte Way. Now turn right down a path aiming for Leeming Reservoir. It descends rough pastures to trace a wall down above Stony Hill Clough. Emerging onto a broader path at the bottom, turn left over a bridge and follow the path away, soon forking right on emerging from trees to drop down to a footbridge. The path runs outside the reservoir wall, deflected by trees and on a largely enclosed course to join an access road in a field. Turn down this, absorbing another drive and down to a junction by the dam. Cross straight over, an enclosed path dropping to Egypt House and out on its access road past cottages at Back Leeming onto a road. Go straight on, dropping down to the start.

Leeming Reservoir

3¹4 miles from Cock Hill

A high-level tramp on good moorland tracks

Start Hebden Bridge road (GR: 013330), parking area on left just below road

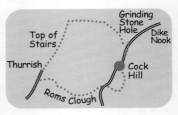

summit above Waggon & Horses at Dike Nook, Oxenhope
Map OS Explorer OL21, South Pennines
Access Open Access land, see page 5

The walk's starting point is, at a lofty 1417ft/432m, its highest point! From the parking area you could simply walk south along the road summit to the University of Bradford's Field Site, but it is more interesting to take a grassy path leaving the rear of the parking area through an old gate, and off across the grassy moor. Ahead is Ovenden Moor windfarm. The path veers right, rising slightly, then deflected further right by peaty ground as it fades after only a few minutes. Here bear off right over intermittently moist ground, aiming for the station mast. Turn left with the perimeter fence, interrupted part way by a fence. Go left 50 strides to a stile, and joining a thin trod just beyond, double back right on it to meet the perimeter fence corner. This quickly leads along to the road, with big views over the head of Crimsworth Dean backed by a long Calderdale moorland skyline.

Cross straight over to a gate from where a grass track descends the grassy moor above Halfpenny Hole Clough. It curves down to a gate above Roms Clough to leave the moor, then curves right around a sweeping pasture, and above a barn. Dropping down over a stone-arched bridge it runs on to Whitehole Farm. Entering the yard take the gate ahead above the main buildings, and a track heads away to merge with the farm drive to run along to a surfaced road. By now Stoodley Pike has appeared far across Calderdale. Turn right up the steeply climbing strip of tarmac, which quickly ends as an access road turns left to Thurrish Farm. Ignore this and continue straight up, now an enclosed track that offers good sections of stone causey as it rises to a gate onto a corner of moorland.

Back in open country the track rises with a wall, and when this turns off taking a stony branch with it, remain on your directly ascending, nicer continuation. This climbs steeply before easing out as a fence brings the wall back in. Advance on a much nicer surface now as the wall leads across the broad watershed at around 1394ft/425m on Top of Stairs. On a clear day the high Wharfedale fells of Great Whernside and Buckden Pike appear ahead, while an inscribed boundary stone stands by the wall. The track starts to drop and descends to a gate alongside a distinctive scarred hollow.

Continue down a little more until crossing a water conduit in a stone channel. Here turn sharp right on an inviting grass track which runs a sustained level course alongside the drain. This gentle promenade offers grand views over Bronte Country, featuring Leeshaw Reservoir, Haworth Moor, Penistone Hill and Oxenhope. Towards the end it swings in around the bracken-filled gulch of Grinding Stone Hole before reaching a gate back onto the A6033. Turn up the road past a parking area, and within ten minutes you will be back at the start, passing isolated Keeper's Lodge on the way. Looking back, Ingleborough's summit has by now appeared far up the Dales, joining Penyghent which revealed itself a little earlier.

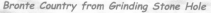

Bronte Country from Grinding Stone Hole

NAB HILL

4 miles from Leeming

A breezy tramp over grassy moors, save it for a clear day

Start Lamb Inn (GR: 037344),
roadside parking nearby
Map OS Explorer OL21,
South Pennines

From the pub advance towards the reservoir and turn right on the road across the dam. At once bear left on a farm road to a fork, where go left across another field. As the farm road climbs away, advance straight on a field-path above the reservoir, quickly becoming largely enclosed. Dropping to a footbridge near the reservoir head, a part embanked path climbs the bank behind to a kissing-gate onto rough grass slopes. The path rises to another kissing-gate at the top, then ascends moor-like slopes, passing a superfluous stone stile before a left fork to a concrete ford. Better to ignore this for the path straight up the gentle spur to soon reach a water conduit. Go left on its green path, around an inlet to quickly reach a stile in a short section of wall at a bridge on the conduit. A thin path rises to trees above to join a track, Sawood Lane.

Turn left, soon winding up between old walls to a firmer wall, with a junction just to the left. Turn right through the gate to ascend Hambleton Lane between old walls. Very shortly escape by a gate on the right, from where the higher of two sunken ways slants across the moor to old quarry spoilheaps. At a crossroads with an edge path, bear right on it: the cairn on Nab Hill beckons further along the edge as the path runs between knolls and abandoned stones. Ovenden Moor windfarm looms across the moor. Beyond the quarry site the path curves around the heads of Little Clough and Great Clough, divided by a moorland edge and a few more remains. It is then a short stroll to Nab Hill's cairn. Set amid further small remains at about 1475ft/450m, this fine specimen has a curved arm incorporating a shelter. The extensive view looks west to Lancashire's Boulsworth Hill and Pendle Hill, while northwards beyond Bronte Country is a panorama of Dales peaks.

From a more capacious shelter on the knoll below, a thin path runs past a ruin to a cairn with triangular arms on marginally higher ground. The thin path then curves left around the slope to drop onto the old quarry track to the left: Warley Moor Reservoir appears ahead. The path curves down beneath spoilheaps to a stile onto Nab Water Lane. You needn't advance to it, instead double back down to a lower stile a little further right. From it a faint path contours across the slope past a tiny pit to a wall corner. Advance along the old walltop, and at the third descending wall drop to a kissing-gate on a conduit, then down through bridle-gates onto the road. Turn right, passing the start of Sawood Lane and on as far as a bend left. From a gate in front head away on an enclosed track, Isle Lane. This emerges into the open to descend a sunken course, with an optional grass track on its right. At the bottom it becomes fully enclosed again, descending pleasantly to the rear of a couple of houses. Go left on the track which slants down onto a surfaced road. Turn right down this between the houses, and where it turns sharp right leave by an enclosed green way on the left. This drops to Egypt House, just before which a stile on the right sends an enclosed path back up to the dam to finish.   *On Nab Hill*

*4³⁄4 miles
from Hainworth*

**A riot of moorland colour
amongst the pastures**

*Start Hamlet centre (GR:
059391), roadside parking
Map OS Explorer OL21, South Pennines
Access Open Access land, see page 5*

From the square head west on unsurfaced Hill Top Road, passing the last cottages and along to a fork. Remain on the higher one, narrowing to a bridleway after another house and on to an old quarry. An enclosed path turns up its near side, through colourful terrain to rise to a house. Its drive rises to a brow then out onto a road. Go briefly left, and from a gate/stile on the right a grassy way descends a slim pasture to a corner stile. Continue down as far as a recess where a gate sends a track to Lower Heights. Follow the drive out, but after a sharp right bend turn into a stable-yard on the left, crossing to a stile onto a road. Turn down for a few minutes and escape left on an enclosed track onto the base of Catstones Moor.

Advance along the full length, and from a gate/stile at the end the way runs beneath a small wood and above a house. Just beyond is a fork: keep to the higher path on an embanked course to a stile onto Ryecroft Road. Cross to a rough road into the neat hamlet of Ryecroft. At the end, in front of Ryecroft Farm, take the left fork out along a fieldside above a side valley. Reaching a lone house, the path runs left above it and into woodland, quickly rising to a stile onto Harden Moor. A super path rises through the bilberry bushes: soon reaching a T-junction, turn right. Ignoring branches this splendid path runs a largely level course, gravitating towards a wall on the right to trace the moor edge to a corner. The wall turns right but your way bears left, through a few boulders then on another grand course along the modest rim of a woodland drop on the right. At the end a kissing-gate puts you onto a broader track, with a house ahead. Turn left, rising close by a wall to a corner. While the wallside track along to the right is the easiest option, nicer to take an early kissing-gate in the fence on your left. A good path slants up to a cluster of boulders to meet a broader path, and bears right across the heart of the moor.

You soon drop slightly to a path crossroads. Turn right, enjoying a slight rise on a super, largely flagged old way to another moor corner, where a kissing-gate re-unites you with the track on the right. At this junction go straight ahead on a broad access road leaving the moor to drop steadily down, ignoring a crossroads and becoming surfaced before joining a road. Drop briefly right then swing left on rougher surfaced Woodhouse Road, with a bird's-eye view over Keighley. Quickly leave by a drive on the left to a lone house. In the yard corner is a wall-stile, from where head away with a wall to a small gate and stile at the far end. Go right a few strides with the wall in front, and at the outer corner follow it away left: further on, pass through a gate after the wall ends and a faint path runs to a stile ahead. In improved condition the thin path heads away with a wall to a corner stile, then on to meet a hard track. Advance on this through an equestrian establishment to re-enter Hainworth.

On Harden Moor

43

**4³₄ miles
from Cullingworth**

**A brilliantly colourful walk
and a lovely waterfall**

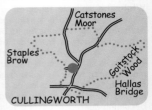

*Start Station Road
(GR: 066368), behind church
Map OS Explorer OL21, South Pennines*

Ascend Station Road to a scattered junction, then go
straight up over the old rail bridge. Across, turn right on another
rough lane which later turns left to rise to houses at Cullingworth
Fields Farm. Here turn right on a more inviting enclosed path,
opening out at a small wood. Remain on the main path rising left
along the top to join an enclosed way at Staples Brow. Turn right
down its pleasant course and along to a gate at the end. Cross a
field to Sugden House, through a gate between buildings and onto
another track. Go left down across a bridge on a tiny stream, but
as the drive swings left go straight ahead over open ground to an
iron ladder-stile, ascending a scrubby bank then up an enclosure to
a drive at Cliffe View. Turn right on this past the house and on
between trees to emerge into a field: the pathless way runs a
straight wallside course through the fields. At the end it drops
down over a sidestream, then up a walled course onto Keighley Road.

Rise left a short way then take an enclosed track on the
right onto the base of Catstones Moor. Advance along as far as the
arrival of Dolphin Lane, an enclosed bridleway on the right.
Engulfed in undergrowth it descends grandly to the B6429: go
right past Cow House Farm as far as a bus stop opposite. Here a
stile sends a wallside path off above the side valley of Cow House
Beck, soon entering scattered trees. Just prior to a big open
pasture, a stile sends the official path over the wall, only to return
to the commonly used path at another stile before reaching the far
end. From a stile on the left between gates the path heads away
outside the wood. Through an old wall it swings left away from the

wood and across a large sloping pasture to a chimney. This served a flue drawing fumes from a steam powered mill below. Just past it is a stile onto a broad path above trees. Double back right down this to the edge of a caravan site.

Reaching a drive, go left a few strides to a panel telling the story of 'Happy Valley', then without crossing the bridge into the site, turn right on a beckside path to a bridge over it, meeting the end of an access road in front of a house. Turn right on a broad path into Goitstock Wood for a lovely walk upstream with Harden Beck. This hugely attractive section passes the confluence of Cow House Beck beneath a craggy knoll before steeper slopes close in to reach Goit Stock Falls, beautiful centrepiece of these woods. A handrail assists in surmounting the little cliff before resuming past a smaller waterfall to Hallas Bridge. Just upstream is the converted Hallas Mill. Cross the bridge and follow the old road's steep, enclosed course to ease out at Hallas Hall Farm. Remain on this past housing onto the B6144 on the village edge. Cross and head up an enclosed way rising to bridge the old railway. Drop onto this and follow it right back towards the centre, quickly reaching a terminus where you are nudged right down to a small road by a school. Don't join but take the path signed to Station Road: it runs firmly on between old line and school, opening out into playing fields at the end then on between houses to Station Road.

Goit Stock Falls

4¾ miles from Denholme

**A wealth of features
in unlikely environs**

*Start Village centre
(GR: 071340), junction of
Foster Park with main road
Map OS Explorer OL21, South Pennines*

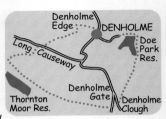

Turn down the road, Foster Park, and straight on down
Foster Park View with the park on your right, leaving the houses
and becoming rougher to drop to Doe Park Reservoir. Across the
dam, turn a few strides right then take a small gate on the left.
Turn right on a path beneath a scrubby bank outside the grounds
of a house. At the end it continues in pleasanter vein through a
sloping pasture above the reservoir. Through a small gate at the
end take another one just a few steps further from where the path
runs an enclosed course, emerging to turn right to a footbridge at
the reservoir head. Up through a stile behind, turn left to drop
back into the valley of Denholme Beck, and an initially moist section
beneath a scrubby bank improves to reach a former Keighley to
Queensbury railway underpass.

An improved continuation traces the small beck up
through colourful Denholme Clough, finally crossing it to run on to
a kissing-gate at the head. Enclosed with the stream the path runs
on to merge onto a drive, continue up onto the A644. Go briefly left
and turn right up Cragg Lane. Almost at once a path turns right up
a narrow snicket, passing between houses to rise into a field.
Continue up with a wall on the right, and from a stile at a cross-wall
rise left on a flagged wallside path to steps up onto the A629 at
Denholme Gate. Cross and go left a few strides to turn up the
unsurfaced Black Edge Lane. This remains your course for a good
mile and a half, rising gradually to Thornton Moor where it becomes
known as Thornton Moor Road. Increasingly extensive views see

Ovenden Moor windfarm over to the left, and a big northerly panorama featuring Ingleborough and Penyghent.

Striding on beneath unseen Thornton Moor Reservoir, the way angles gently down to become surfaced at an access road junction beneath a house. Turn right just as far as a sharp bend left, and leave by a gate on the right. A grass track crosses a rough pasture to a gate into a field, running a slightly embanked course with a wall on your right. At the end bear left on a wallside track out to the B6141. Go right a short way then escape via an iron turn-stile at ornate gates on the left. An old way heads away towards a house in trees ahead, going left to find another gate/turnstile into the head of Pit Lane. Follow this enclosed track along the rear of fine buildings until a wooden barn on the left: turn left here up a short-lived walled cart track. At the end take a stile on the right and resume your line along a fieldside, with a wall on your left. The way drops to a corner stile on the rim of Denholme Edge, with Hewenden Reservoir and Hewenden Viaduct seen ahead. Turn right, a grand path tracing the crest of this open bank, through a small gate at the end onto the best section, bedecked in heather and overlooking modern housing. Amble along to the end, tapering to become a track running out onto the main road at Edge Bottom. With the New Inn just to the left, cross and turn right to finish.

Doe Park Reservoir

HILLSIDE GUIDES... cover much of Northern England

Short Scenic Walks guides (more in preparation)

·UPPER WHARFEDALE ·LOWER WHARFEDALE
·UPPER WENSLEYDALE ·LOWER WENSLEYDALE
·MALHAMDALE ·SWALEDALE ·RIBBLESDALE
·INGLETON/WESTERN DALES ·SEDBERGH/DENTDALE
·NIDDERDALE ·HARROGATE/KNARESBOROUGH
·BOWLAND ·AROUND PENDLE ·RIBBLE VALLEY
·BORROWDALE ·HAWORTH/BRONTE COUNTRY
·ILKLEY/WASHBURN VALLEY ·AMBLESIDE/LANGDALE
·AIRE VALLEY ·HEBDEN BRIDGE/CALDER VALLEY

Our *Walking Country* range features longer walks...

·WHARFEDALE ·MALHAMDALE ·WENSLEYDALE
·HARROGATE & the WHARFE VALLEY ·SWALEDALE
·RIPON & LOWER WENSLEYDALE ·NIDDERDALE
·THREE PEAKS ·HOWGILL FELLS ·HOWARDIAN HILLS
·TEESDALE ·EDEN VALLEY ·ALSTON & ALLENDALE

·ILKLEY MOOR ·BRONTE COUNTRY ·CALDERDALE
·PENDLE & the RIBBLE ·WEST PENNINE MOORS
·ARNSIDE & SILVERDALE ·LUNESDALE ·BOWLAND

·LAKELAND FELLS, SOUTH ·LAKELAND FELLS, EAST
·LAKELAND FELLS, NORTH ·LAKELAND FELLS, WEST

Long Distance Walks

·COAST TO COAST WALK ·CUMBRIA WAY ·DALES WAY
·NIDDERDALE WAY ·FURNESS WAY ·CALDERDALE WAY
·WESTMORLAND WAY ·PENDLE WAY ·BRONTE WAY

Visit www.hillsidepublications.co.uk
or write for a catalogue
